THE SILK DRAGON: TRANSLATIONS FROM THE CHINESE

TRANSLATIONS FROM THE CHINESE

The Silk Dragon

Arthur Sze

COPPER CANYON PRESS

Printed in the United States of America.

Cover image: *Nine Dragons* (detail), China, Southern Song dynasty, dated 1244, Chen Rong, handscroll; ink and touches of red on paper, Francis Gardner Curtis Fund, 1917. Courtesy, Museum of Fine Arts, Boston.

Copper Canyon Press is in residence under the auspices of the Centrum Foundation at Fort Worden State Park in Port Townsend, Washington. Centrum sponsors artist residencies, education workshops for Washington State students and teachers, blues, jazz, and fiddle tunes festivals, classical music performances, and The Port Townsend Writers' Conference.

LIBRARY OF CONGRESS CATALOGING-IN-PUBLICATION DATA

Sze, Arthur.

The silk dragon: translations from the Chinese / Arthur Sze.

p. cm.

Includes bibliographical references and index.

ISBN 1-55659-153-5

1. Chinese poetry — Translations into English.

1. Title: Translations of Chinese poetry. 11. Title.

PL2658.E3 S9 2000

895.1'1008 — DC21

2001002044

3 5 7 9 8 6 4 2

FIRST PRINTING

COPPER CANYON PRESS

Post Office Box 271

Port Townsend, Washington 98368

www.coppercanyonpress.org

Grateful acknowledgment is made to the editors of the following publications in which these poems, sometimes in earlier versions, first appeared:

The Bloomsbury Review: "Drinking Wine (I)."

Bombay Gin: "Drinking Alone with the Moon," "To the Tune of 'Meeting Happiness.'"

Buttons: "Return to Chiang Village," "Spring View."

Columbia: "Moonlight Night," "Easing My Heart," "On the Willow Bank."

Denver Quarterly: "Drinking Wine (III)," "A Question Addressed to Mr. Liu," "To the Tune of 'Joy in the Oriole's Flight.'"

First Intensity: "Bamboo Grove," "Deer Park," "Hsin-yi Village," "The Brocade Zither," "Untitled (I)," "The Lo-yu Tombs," "On a Rainy Night, Lines to Be Sent North."

Gate (Germany): "Untitled," "Highland," "Song of Ch'ang-kan," "Night Thoughts," "The Lotus," "To the Tune of 'Clear Happiness.'"

Green Mountains Review: "Night at the Tower," "Autumn Comes."

Hanging Loose: "Snow on the River," "Anchored at Ch'in-huai River."

The Kenyon Review: "Untitled (II)," "Inscribed on a Painting," "Globefish," "Inscription for a Painting," "Bright Light and Cloud Shadows."

Luna: "Bamboo," "From a Painting of a Cat."

Malini: "Dead Water."

Manoa: the introductory essay appeared under the title "Translating a Poem by Li Shang-yin."

New Letters: "Song of the Collator's Sword in the Spring Bureau."

The New Mexican: "Drinking Wine (I)."

Pax: "Drinking Wine (II)," "Returning to Fields and Gardens (I) and (II)," "To the Tune of 'Intoxicated in the Shadows of Flowers.'"

The Portsmouth Review: "Sending Off Mr. Yuan," "To the Tune of 'Telling My Most Intimate Feelings,'" "The Last Day."

The Santa Fe Reporter: "To the Tune of 'Sky-clear Sand': Autumn Thoughts."

Sol Tide: "The Lotus," "Good Harvest," "The Plum Hint," "Red Rain."

Stooge: "Song of Liang-chou."

Tarasque: "To the Tune of 'Plum Blossoms in the Breeze': Evening Bell at a Misty Temple," "To the Tune of 'Sky-clear Sand': Autumn Thoughts," "Dead Water," "Perhaps," "Miracle."

2 Plus 2 (Switzerland): "To the Tune of 'Sailing at Night' (I) and (II)," "To the Tune of 'Sky-clear Sand': Autumn Thoughts."

Volt: "Flying Light."

The World: "Spring Night."

Anthology of Magazine Verse & Yearbook of American Poetry (Monitor, 1985): "Drinking Wine (I)."

Literatures of Asia, Africa, and Latin America (Prentice Hall, 1999): "Miracle."

Poems for the Millennium (University of California Press, 1995): "Dead Water," "Miracle."

World Poetry (Norton, 1998): "Flying Light," "Untitled (I)," "To the Tune of 'Meeting Happiness,'" "Dead Water," "On the Willow Bank."

"Drinking Alone with the Moon" appeared as a broadside from Lumen Books.

Some of these translations also appeared in *The Willow Wind* (Tooth of Time, 1981) and *Two Ravens* (Tooth of Time, 1984).

I wish to thank the Witter Bynner Foundation for Poetry and the Lila Wallace–Reader's Digest Fund for their support.

for my parents,
Morgan C.Y. Sze & Agnes C. Lin Sze

Contents

THE SILK DRAGON: TRANSLATIONS FROM THE CHINESE

Introduction

The translation of Chinese poems into English has always been a source of inspiration for my own evolution as a poet. In 1971, as a student at the University of California at Berkeley, I majored in poetry. Also studying Chinese language and literature, I became interested in translating the great T'ang-dynasty poets — Li Po, Tu Fu, Wang Wei, among others — because I felt I could learn from them. I felt that by struggling with many of the great poems in the Chinese literary tradition, I could best develop my voice as a poet. Years later, in 1983, after publishing *Dazzled,* my third book of poetry, I translated a new group of Chinese poems, again feeling that it would help me discern greater possibilities for my own writing. I was drawn to the clarity of T'ao Ch'ien's lines, to the subtlety of Ma Chih-yüan's lyrics, and to Wen I-to's sustained, emotional power. In 1996, after completing my book *Archipelago,* I felt the need to translate yet another group of Chinese poems: I was particularly drawn to the Ch'an-influenced work of Pa-ta-shan-jen and to the extremely condensed and challenging, transformational poems of Li Ho and Li Shang-yin.

I know translation is an "impossible" task, and I have never forgotten the Italian phrase *traduttori/traditori:* "translators/traitors." Which translation does not in some way betray its original? In considering the process of my own translations, I am aware of loss and transformation, of destruction and renewal. Since I first started to write poetry, I have only translated poems that have deeply engaged me; and it has sometimes taken me many years to feel ready to work on one. I remember that in 1972 I read Li Shang-yin's untitled poems and felt baffled by them; now, more than twenty-five years later, his verses—veiled, mysterious, and full of longing—strike me as some of the great love poems in classical Chinese.

To show how I create a translation in English, I am going to share stages and drafts of a translation from one of Li Shangyin's untitled poems. I like to begin by writing the Chinese characters out on paper. I know that my own writing of Chinese is awkward and rudimentary, but, by writing out the characters in their particular stroke order, I can begin to sense the inner motion of the poem in a way that I cannot by just reading the characters on the page. Once I've written out the characters, I look up each in Robert H. Mathews's *Chinese-English Dictionary* and write down the sound and tone along with a word, phrase, or cluster of words that helps mark its field of energy and meaning. I go through the entire poem doing this groundwork. After I have created this initial cluster of words, I go back through and, because a Chinese character can mean so many different things depending on its context, I remove words or phrases that appear to be inappropriate and keep those that appear to be relevant. In the case of Li Shang-yin's untitled poem, I now have a draft that looks like the figure on the facing page.

In looking at this regulated eight-line poem, I know that each of its seven-character lines has two predetermined caesuras, so that the motion in Chinese is 1-2 / 3-4 / 5-6-7. I try to catch the tonal flow and sense the silences. I know that the tones from Mathews's dictionary only give me the barest approximation. T'ang-dynasty poems are most alive when they are chanted. The sounds are very different from the Mandarin dialect that I speak. Yet I can, for instance, guess that the sound

鳳	尾	香	羅	薄	幾	重
male phoenix feng⁴	*tail/s* wei³	*fragrant* hsiang¹	*gauze, thin silk* lo²	*thin, slight* po²	*how many* chi³	*layers, folds* ch'ung²
碧	文	圓	頂	夜	深	逢
green jade pi⁴	*elegant, refined* wen²	*round* yüan²	*the top* ting³	*night* yeh⁴	*deep* shen¹	*meet with* feng²
扇	裁	月	魄	羞	難	掩
fan shan⁴	*to cut* ts'ai²	*moon* yüeh⁴	*form, shape* p'o⁴	*shame, blush* hsiu¹	*difficult* nan²	*conceal* yen³
車	走	雷	聲	語	未	通
carriage ch'e¹	*departs* tsou³	*thunder* lei²	*sound/s* sheng¹	*word/s* yü³	*not yet* wei⁴	*get through* t'ung¹
曾	是	寂	寥	金	燼	暗
once, already ts'eng²	*is* shih⁴	*silent* chi⁴	*empty* liao²	*gold* chin¹	*ashes, embers* chin⁴	*dark, cloudy* an⁴
斷	無	消	息	石	榴	紅
cut off tuan⁴	*no, without* wu²	*— ebb and flow —* hsiao¹	hsi²	*— pomegranate —* shih²	liu²	*red* hung²
班	騅	只	繫	垂	楊	柳
mottled pan¹	*piebald horse* chui¹	*only, but* chih³	*tie, bind* hsi⁴	*hang down* ch'ui²	*— willow —* yang²	liu³
何	處	西	南	任	好	風
what, which ho²	*place* ch'u⁴	*— southwest —* hsi¹	nan²	*allow, confide in* jen⁴	*good* hao³	*wind* feng¹

of *tuan*[4], the first character in line six, is sharp and emphatic. I also sense that characters three and four in line six — *hsiao*[1] and *hsi*[2] — have an onomatopoeic quality to suggest ebb and flow. In double-checking this phrase in the dictionary, I realize it has the primary meaning of "news and information"; there is no news, and the speaker is in a state of heightened isolation. In looking at the visual configuration of the characters, I am again struck by the first character in line six, *tuan*[4]. Here the character contains the image of scissors cutting silk, and I wonder if this can be extended to develop an insight into the poem.

I proceed by writing a rough draft in English: trying to write eight lines in English that are equivalent to the eight lines in Chinese. I realize immediately that the translation is too cramped. I look back at the Chinese and decide to use *two* lines in English for each line of Chinese. I also decide to emphasize the second caesura of each line in Chinese so that in English there's a line break after the meaning of the fourth character in each line of the Chinese original.

I write out another draft in which sixteen lines in English now stand for the eight lines in Chinese. All of the lines in English are flush left, but the blocklike form does not do justice to the obliquely cutting motion of the poem. To open it up and clarify the architecture, I decide to indent all of the even-numbered lines. I go through another series of drafts, which oftentimes incorporate English words that I've listed on the page with Chinese characters, though I don't feel compelled to use all of them. At this transitional stage, I have something that looks like the following version (without any of the crossed-out or underlined words):

phoenix tails, fragrant silk,
⌐*folds*
how many thin ~~layers~~.

under the ~~elegant~~ green round canopy
⌐*opens to*
she ~~encounters~~ the deep night.

the fan cuts the moon's shape
⌐*but*   ⌐*blush*
~~and~~ can't conceal her ~~shame~~.

a carriage goes, thunder sounds,
⌐*didn't*
the words ~~can't~~ get through.

a while in the desolate quiet
✕ ═══════

gold embers in the dark.
nothing now but   ⌐*the ebb and flow of*
↳ ~~cut off, no word, who could be pouring~~

~~a measure of~~ red pomegranate wine?

a piebald horse is yet tied
⌐*dangling*
to a ~~trailing~~ willow.
⌐*from*
and where is the place ~~in~~ the southwest
✕ ═══════════

where the fine breeze can blow?

At this point, if there are books of Chinese translations that
I think might be helpful, I look at them to see if they have any
commentaries that are relevant. In François Cheng's *Chinese*

Poetic Writing I find that lines one and two "describe the bed-curtain of a bridal chamber," that "to pluck a willow branch" means to visit a courtesan, that red pomegranate wine might be served at a wedding feast and connotes explosive desire, and that the southwest breeze alludes to a phrase by Ts'ao Chih (192–232), "I would become that southwest wind / waft all the way to your bosom." I find these comments insightful but do not want to incorporate them overtly into my translation. Because Li Shang-yin's great strength is his oblique exactitude, I want my translation to hint at these elements.

I now look at my very rough translation and go back to the original Chinese. My experience of the poem is that a solitary woman is lamenting the absence of her lover and longs for him even as she worries that he is unfaithful. I go back through my translation, cross out certain phrases, and substitute new phrases wherever they seem better. With the second line, I decide that it is more appropriate to have the silk in folds than in layers. In line three, the phrase "elegant green round canopy" is cumbersome; I decide the word "elegant" is too stated and should be removed. It's so hard in a contemporary poem to use an adjective like "elegant" and not cause a boomerang effect. I read on and decide that "encounters" is too neutral. To make the longing more overt, I change it to "opens to the deep night." In line six, I change "and" to "but," and substitute "blush" for "shame." I'm happy with this last change: the "blush" will help foreshadow the "red pomegranate wine" and also suggests the red of desire. In line eight, I change "can't" to "didn't," though I'm not sure this is better. In line nine, I mark with an *x* and double-underline the word "desolate". This word is another loaded adjective, but nothing comes to mind as a good replacement, so I mark it with an *x* to tell myself to come back to it. I am totally dissatisfied with line eleven and strike it out. I go back to the page with characters and reincorporate "ebb and flow." With line fourteen, I am uneasy about "trailing" and insert "dangling." Line fifteen strikes me as too wordy, but again nothing comes to mind, so I mark it with an *x* and a double-underline.

At this point, I put the translation away for a few weeks. I brood on it and, if some changes come to mind, jot them down on the side. But I usually wait until I'm ready to revise with intensity and clarity. When I finally sit down and rework the translation, I decide that "the deep quiet" opens up the emotional space in a way that "the desolate quiet" can't. I decide to foreground the gold embers and make them a more active presence; the verb "scintillate" leaps into my mind. To suggest that red pomegranate wine connotes explosive desire, and to make the configuration of sounds more alive, I replace the static "a measure of red pomegranate wine" with the active "pulsing red pomegranate wine." I also decide to break the symmetry of the indented lines by further indenting the very last line; I think this heightens the cutting effect of the ending. You can see these significant changes incorporated into the final version:

UNTITLED (II) *by Li Shang-yin*

Phoenix tails, fragrant silk,
      so many thin folds.
Under the round green canopy,
      she opens herself to the night.
A fan cuts the moon's shape

but can't conceal her blush.
The carriage goes, thunder sounds;
   the words couldn't get through.
A while in the deep quiet,
   gold embers scintillate:
nothing now but the ebb and flow of
   pulsing red pomegranate wine.
A piebald horse is yet tied
   to a dangling willow.
And where out of the southwest
    can the fine breeze blow?

I hope going through this poem at length shows how arduous but also how rewarding the process of translation can be. *The Silk Dragon* presents in English the work of eighteen poets presented in chronological order, beginning with T'ao Ch'ien (365–427) and ending with Yen Chen, who published in the 1950s. It is a collection of personal favorites; yet, slim as it is, I hope it presents a complex vision of the vitality, diversity, and power of the Chinese poetic tradition.

Many American readers are by now familiar with Li Po, Wang Wei, and Tu Fu, but too few readers know Li Ho, Li Shang-yin, Ma Chih-yüan, Shen Chou, Pa-ta-shan-jen, Wen I-to, or Yen Chen. There exists a huge gulf in many readers' awareness between the early T'ang poets and the contemporary Misty School poets. There is no way a small volume such as this can fill in those gaps, but I want to single out poems of particular excellence that can serve as landmarks. And where I have chosen a single poem by a poet, it is in no way an indication that the poet merits only one poem in this anthology; it is merely that I have only been able to make one translation with which I am satisfied.

This collection assembles all of the translations I consider finished; because there is a poet who lived as early as 400 C.E., and because I have relied so heavily on Mathews's *Chinese-English Dictionary,* I have used the Wade-Giles romanization system.

There are several people I want to thank for help with these translations. In 1971 Ts'ai Mei-hsi taught conversational Mandarin at the University of California at Berkeley; I was in one of his classes, and he generously agreed to help me review poems by Li Po, Tu Fu, Wang Wei, and also introduced me to Yen Chen's work. In 1983 Pan Chia-hsiu helped me with the T'ao Ch'ien, Li Ch'ing-chao, Ma Chih-yüan, and Wen I-to. In recent years, Xue Di helped me with a poem by Li Ho, and Yang Hsiao-hui helped me with another by Li Shang-yin. Because many of the Li Ho and Li Shang-yin poems have difficult allusions, I have appended notes at the end of the book to clarify them.

In closing, I want to mention my idea that the mind is a dragon. In Chinese culture, a dragon embodies magic, transformation, and energy. Wolfram Eberhard once wrote, "As a magic animal, the dragon is able to shrink to the size of a silkworm; and then it can swell up till it fills the space between heaven and earth." Li Shang-yin wrote in a famous untitled poem, included in this collection, "A spring silkworm spins silk / up to the instant of death." That phrase can be taken as a metaphor for how a poet works with language. "The silk dragon," then, is my metaphor for poetry.

ARTHUR SZE

Drinking Wine (1)

A green pine is in the east garden,
but the many grasses obscure it.
A frost wipes out all the other species,
and then I see its magnificent tall branches.
In a forest men do not notice it, but
standing alone, it is a miracle.
I hang a jug of wine on a cold branch;
then stand back, and look again and again.
My life spins with dreams and illusions.
Why then be fastened to the world?

Drinking Wine (11)

I built my house near where others live,
and yet without noise of horse or carriage.
You ask, how can this be?
A distant mind leaves the earth around it.
I pick chrysanthemums below the eastern fence,
then gaze at mountains to the south.
The mountain air is fine at sunset;
flying birds go back in flocks.
In this there is a truth;
I wish to tell you, but lose the words.

Drinking Wine (III)

Fall chrysanthemums have fine colors.
I pluck a few blossoms speckled with dew
and float one in wine to forget my sorrow
and leave the world far behind.
Alone, I pour myself a cup, but when
it's empty, the jug tips and refills it.
At dusk, all movement slows to a stop.
The birds fly back to the woods, singing.
I whistle and whistle on the east veranda—
go ahead, embrace this life!

Returning to Fields and Gardens (1)

When I was young, I did not fit in
with others, and simply loved the hills and mountains.
By mistake, I fell into the dusty net
and before I knew it, it was thirty years!
The caged bird longs for the old forest.
The fish in the pond misses the old depths.
I cultivate land along the southern wilds,
and, keeping to simplicity, return to fields and gardens.
Ten acres now surround my house;
it is thatched, and has eight, nine rooms.
Elms and willows shade the back eaves.
Peach and plum trees are lined out the front hall.
The distant village is hazy, hazy: and
slender, slender, the smoke hanging over houses.
Dogs bark in the deep lane, and a rooster
crows on top of a mulberry tree.
My house untouched by the dust of the world—
ample leisure in these bare rooms.
I was held so long inside a narrow bird-
cage, but now, at last, can return to nature.

Returning to Fields and Gardens (II)

I plant beans below the southern hill:
there grasses flourish and bean sprouts are sparse.
At dawn, I get up, clear out a growth of weeds,
then go back, leading the moon, a hoe over my shoulder.

Now the path is narrow, grasses and bushes are high.
Evening dew moistens my clothes;
but so what if my clothes are wet—
I choose not to avoid anything that comes.

Song of Liang-chou

The grape wine is beautiful
as light shines into the cup at night.
I would like to drink
but the lute urges me to mount my horse.
Sir, if I am lying drunk on the battlefield,
please do not laugh.
Since ancient times,
how many soldiers ever returned?

Bamboo Grove

I sit alone in the secluded bamboo grove
and play the zither and whistle along.
In the deep forest no one knows,
the bright moon comes to shine on me.

Deer Park

The mountain is empty, no man can be seen;
but the echo of human sounds is heard.
Returning sunlight, entering the deep forest,
shines again on green moss, above.

Hsin-yi Village

At the tips of branches,
  hibiscus
opening red calyxes
  deep in the mountains.
A stream, hut:
  yet no one.
The flowers bloom
  and fall, bloom and fall.

WANG WEI

Untitled

Sir, you come from my native home
and should know the affairs there.
The day you left, beside the silk-paned window—
did the cold plum sprout flowers or not?

Highland

Peach blossom's red, filled with night rain.
The willow, green,
is still veiled in the mist of spring.
The boy has not swept up the fallen petals.
Orioles singing,
the mountain hermit is yet sleeping.

Sending Off Mr. Yuan

The rain settles a light dust in Wei City.
Green, green are the willows by the traveler's hut.
Sir, I advise you to empty another cup of wine,
for west of Yang Pass you will meet no friend.

Drinking Alone with the Moon

Among the flowers with a jug of wine,
I pour, alone, lacking companions,
and, raising cup, invite the bright moon:
facing my shadow makes three people.
But the moon is unable to drink,
and my shadow just follows my body;
for a time, the moon leads the shadow—
be joyous as long as it's spring!
I sing, and the moon wavers.
I dance, and the shadow stumbles.
When sober, we were intimate friends;
now drunk, each of us separates.
May we be bound and travel without anxieties—
may we meet in the far Milky Way.

Song of Ch'ang-kan

When my hair just began to cover my forehead,
I was plucking flowers, playing in front of the gate.
You came along riding a bamboo stick horse,
circling and throwing green plums.
Together we lived in Ch'ang-kan Village
never suspicious of our love.
At fourteen, I became your wife,
my shy face never opened.
I lowered my head, faced the dark wall,
to your thousand calls, never a response.
At fifteen, I became enlightened,
was willing to be dust with you, ashes with you.
Always preserving you in my heart,
why should I ascend the terrace to look for your return?
At sixteen, you traveled far, through
Chü-t'ang Gorge, by rocks and swirling waters...
And in the fifth month, they are impassable,
monkeys wailing to the sky...
By our door where you left footprints,
mosses, one by one, grew over;

too deep to be swept away!

Leaves fall early in the autumn wind.

In lunar August, yellow butterflies

hovered in pairs over the west garden grasses.

My heart hurt at this sight, beauty flickering...

Sooner or later, if you return through the Three Pa district,

send home first. I will meet you,

ignore the long distance, even to Long Wind Sands.

Night Thoughts

The moonlight falls by my bed.
I wonder if there's frost on the ground.
I raise my head to look at the moon,
then ease down, thinking of home.

The Lotus

Lotus flowers blossomed, and the river was drenched in red.
Sir, you said the lotuses were more beautiful than me.
Yesterday, when I passed by the flowers,
why, then, didn't people look at the lotus?

To the Tune of "Clear Happiness"

Clouds remind me of her dress
and flowers of her face.
The spring wind caresses the rail
where dew clusters
on the blossoms.
If you do not see her majesty
on the top of Jade Mountain,
perhaps you will meet her
(as the moon sinks)
on the Green Jasper Terrace.

TU FU

Return to Chiang Village

Shaggy red clouds in the west—
the sun's foot is down to level earth.
By the wicker gate, sparrows are chirping.
The traveler returns from over a thousand *li*.

Wife and children panic at my presence;
quieted, they still wipe tears.
In this age of turmoil, I floated and meandered.
A miracle of chance to return alive!

Neighbors crowd the fence tops
and also sigh and sob.
In the deep night, we are again holding candles,
facing each other as in a dream.

Spring View

The nation is broken, but hills and rivers remain.
Spring is in the city, grasses and trees are thick.
Touched by the hard times, flowers shed tears.
Grieved by separations, birds are startled in their hearts.

The beacon fires burned for three consecutive months.
A letter from home would be worth ten thousand pieces
       of gold.
As I scratch my white head, the hairs become fewer:
so scarce that I try in vain to fasten them with a pin.

Night at the Tower

At year's end, yin and yang
>hasten the shortening daylight.
Frost and snow at the sky's edge
>clear into a crisp, cold night.
At fifth watch, drums and bugles
>sound a piercing grief,
while over Three Gorges, shadows
>of the Milky Way sway and rock.
In the countryside, wild sobs
>resounded through homes after the destruction.
Here and there, tribal songs
>of fishermen and woodcutters arise.
Lying-Dragon and Leaping-Horse
>have disintegrated into yellow dust;
let the news of all our affairs
>... be still and hushed.

Moonlight Night

This evening in Fu-chou my wife
can only look out alone at the moon.
From Ch'ang-an I pity my children
who cannot yet remember nor understand.

Her hair is damp in the fragrant mist.
Her arms are cold in the clear light.
When will we lean beside the window
and the moon shine on our dried tears?

Thoughts on a Night Journey

A slight wind stirs grasses along the bank.
A lone boat sails with a mast in the night.
The stars are pulled down to the vast plain,
and the moon bobs in the river's flow.

My name will never be famous in literature:
I have resigned office from sickness and age.
Drifting and drifting, what am I
but a solitary gull between earth and heaven?

A Question Addressed to Mr. Liu

I have some newly brewed "green ant" wine
and a small stove made of red clay.
As evening comes, the sky threatens snow:
could we not drink a cup?

LIU TSUNG-YÜAN

Snow on the River

Over thousands of mountains
birds no longer fly.
Over ten thousand paths
no more trace of humans.
On a lone boat, an old man
in a bamboo hat and palm coat,
alone fishing,
in the cold snowy river.

Flying Light

Flying light, flying light—
I urge you to drink a cup of wine.
I do not know the height of blue heaven
or the extent of yellow earth.
I only sense the moon's cold,
sun's burn, sear us.
Eat bear, and you'll grow fat;
eat frog, and you'll waste away.
Where is the Spirit Lady?
And where the Great Unity?
East of the sky is the Jo tree:
underneath, a dragon, torch in mouth.
I will cut off the dragon's feet
and chew the dragon's flesh:
then morning will never return
and evening cannot bend.
Old men will not die
nor young men weep.
Why then swallow yellow gold
or gulp down white jade?

Who is Jen Hung-tzu,

riding a white ass through the clouds?

Liu Ch'e, in Mao-ling tomb, is just a heap of bones.

And Ying Cheng rots in his catalpa coffin,

wasting all that abalone.

Song of the Collator's Sword in the Spring Bureau

Elder, inside your casket
　　　　is three feet of water.
This sword once plunged
　　　　into Wu Lake and beheaded a dragon.
A slash of brightest moonlight
　　　　shaves the cold dew.
A white satin sash lies flat
　　　　and will not ruffle in wind.
The hilt of ancient shark-womb skin
　　　　has bristling caltrops.
A white-breasted seabird
　　　　tempered into a white pheasant's tail.
Truly this is a sliver
　　　　of Ching Ko's heart!
Do not let it shine on
　　　　the characters in the Spring Bureau.
Twisted strands of coiling gold
　　　　hang from the hilt.
The sword's brilliant shine
　　　　can sunder an Indigo Field jade.

Draw, and the White King
        of the West will quake—
wailing and wailing, his demon
        mother in the autumn wilds.

Autumn Comes

Wind in the plane tree startles the heart: a grown man's grief.
By dying lamplight, crickets are weeping cold threads.
Who will ever read the green bamboo slips of this book?
Or stop the ornate worms from gnawing powdery holes?
Such thoughts tonight must disentangle in my gut.
In the humming rain, a fragrant spirit consoles this poet.
On an autumn grave, a ghost chants Pao Chao's poem,
and his spiteful blood, buried a thousand years, is now

      green jade.

Anchored at Ch'in-huai River

Mist veils the cold water,
and moonlight veils the sands.
I anchored at Ch'in-huai
near the wine taverns.
Women singers, not knowing
the agonies of a destroyed nation,
still sing the tune of
"Back Court Flowers" on the farther bank.

Easing My Heart

Ill-fated, I carried wine
while traveling through the world.
Chao Fei-yen's waist was so slender and delicate:
she was weightless in my arms.
For ten years I indulged;
now, in Yang-chou, awaken from my dream:
having gained in the blue houses
only a drifting name.

The Brocade Zither

This brocade zither, for no apparent reason, has fifty strings.

Each string and each bridge bring to mind a blossoming year.

Chuang Tzu had a morning dream of a confused butterfly.

Wang-ti's passion was transformed into a calling cuckoo.

On a vast sea, when the moon is bright, pearls contain tears.

At Indigo Field, when the sun is warm, jade engenders smoke.

This passion might have become a memory to stop time

but is at this instant already dispossessed.

Untitled (1)

The chance to meet is difficult,
>   but parting is even more difficult.
The east wind is powerless
>   as the hundred flowers wither.
A spring silkworm spins silk
>   up to the instant of death.
A candle only stops weeping
>   when its wick becomes ash.
In the morning mirror, she grieves
>   that the hair on her temples whitens.
Chanting poems in the evening,
>   she only senses the moonlight's cold.
From here, P'eng Mountain is not too far.
>   O Green Bird, seek, seek her out.

Untitled (11)

Phoenix tails, fragrant silk,
      so many thin folds.
Under the round green canopy,
      she opens herself to the night.
A fan cuts the moon's shape
      but can't conceal her blush.
The carriage goes, thunder sounds;
      the words couldn't get through.
A while in the deep quiet,
      gold embers scintillate:
nothing now but the ebb and flow of
      pulsing red pomegranate wine.
A piebald horse is yet tied
      to a dangling willow.
And where out of the southwest
      can the fine breeze blow?

The Lo-yu Tombs

Toward evening,
> I was uneasy and restless.

I urged my carriage
> up to an ancient mound.

The setting sun
> was boundlessly beautiful,

but it was
> near the yellow dusk.

On a Rainy Night, Lines to Be Sent North

You ask me when I return, but I know not when.
The pools here at Pa Shan overflow with rain.
When will we trim candles by the western window
and the rain of this evening be in our words?

To the Tune of "Meeting Happiness"

Silent and alone, I ascend the west tower.
The moon is like a hook.
In solitude, the *wu tung* trees
imprison the clear autumn in the deep courtyard.
Scissored but not severed,
trimmed but still massive:
it is the sorrow of parting,
another strange flavor in the heart.

To the Tune of "Joy in the Oriole's Flight"

The dawn moon begins to sink,
and last night's mist dissolves.
Speechless, I toss on my pillow:
my dream is of a return to fragrant grasses
and my thoughts cling, cling to them.
In the distant sky, the geese call once and are gone.

The orioles cry, then scatter,
leaving the last of the blossoms to decay.
I'm terribly alone in the deep court:
do not let the last of the red petals be swept away
but leave them for the dancing girls
to step on as they walk home.

Spring Night

Spring night: one-quarter of an hour
is worth a thousand pieces of gold.
Flowers have clear fragrance;
the moon has shadow.
Songs and flutes on the upstairs terrace;
the threadlike sound is fine, fine.
A rope-swing in the still courtyard,
where night is deep, deep.

To the Tune of "Intoxicated in the Shadows of Flowers"

Thin mist, dense clouds, a grief-stricken day;
auspicious incense burns in the gold animal.
Once again, it is the joyous mid-autumn festival,
but a midnight chill
touches my jade pillow and silk bed-screen.

I drink wine by the eastern fence in the yellow dusk.
Now a dark fragrance fills
my sleeves and makes me spin.
The bamboo blinds sway in the west wind.
And I am even thinner than a yellow flower.

To the Tune of "Telling My Most Intimate Feelings"

When night comes,
>I am so flushed with wine,
I undo my hair slowly:
>a plum calyx is
>>stuck on a damaged branch.
I wake dazed when smoke
>>breaks my spring sleep.
The dream distant,
>so very distant;
>>and it is quiet, so very quiet.
The moon spins and spins.
The kingfisher blinds are drawn;
>and yet I rub the injured bud,
>>and yet I twist in my fingers this fragrance,
>>and yet I possess these moments of time!

To the Tune of "Plum Blossoms in the Breeze": Evening Bell at a Misty Temple

Thin cold smoke,
> old still temple.
Near yellow dusk,
> and all the worshipers gone.
A soft west wind
> sounds the bell three, four times.

How can the old master
> practice *dhyana?*

To the Tune of "Sailing at Night" (1)

When all hope of
  profit and fame is gone,
yes and no, right and wrong
  lose their meanings.
The world no longer
  draws me to the front door.
Green trees lean over
  and shade a corner of the house.
Blue hills fill to perfection
  the space over the wall.
Here is a simple
  bamboo fence and thatched cottage.

To the Tune of "Sailing at Night" (11)

Think of the Ch'in palace
    and Han imperial city.
It is all wilds now
    where oxen and sheep graze.
If it were not like this,
    fishermen and woodcutters would have nothing to say.
North and south, tombs in the wilds.
    East and west, gravestones smashed.
Lying-Dragon and Leaping-Horse
    were once famous generals.
Now it is impossible to distinguish
    dragon from snake on the stones.

To the Tune of "Sky-clear Sand": Autumn Thoughts

Withered vine,
old tree,
crows.

A small bridge,
flowing water,
houses.

Ancient road,
west wind,
lean horse.

Sun sinking
in the west—

and a man,
crushed,
at the sky's edge.

Inscribed on a Painting

White clouds, like a sash,
>
> wind around the mountain's waist.

Stone steps rise into the void
>
> on this steep narrow path.

Alone, leaning on a chenopod staff,
>
> I gaze into the expanse

and wish to respond to the murmuring mountain stream
>
> by playing my bamboo flute.

Globefish

*from the third of four album leaves, where a poem
accompanies each painting*

A fine rain drizzles and drizzles
on Yellow Bamboo Village.
A light boat bobs and bobs
among waves and clouds.
How can you get
a meal of yellow sprouts?
In May, globefish
are swallowed upside-down.

Bamboo

from the last of four album leaves

I sketch bamboo with cinnabar,
yet the cinnabar does not do it.
Just now, above the waters of the Hsiang,
dragonflies, and rosy clouds.

From a Painting of a Cat

Nan Ch'uan wanted to be reborn as a water buffalo,
but who did the body of the malicious cat become?
Black clouds and covering snow are alike.
It took thirty years for clouds to disperse, snow to melt.

Inscription for a Painting

Summer solstice: on Chang-t'ai Street
I dab a corpselike cloud image with a brush.
Of the chronicles recited on the ancient terrace,
where is the wind that will wash them away?

Bright Light and Cloud Shadows

from the first of ten album leaves

Spring mountains have no near or far.
A thought of the past instantly becomes a forest.
With no place where clouds are not flying,
how did a worldly thought come to mind?

Dead Water

Here is a ditch of hopelessly dead water.
A cool breeze would not raise the slightest ripple on it.
You might throw in some scraps of copper and rusty tins,
or dump in as well the remains of your meal.

Perhaps the green on copper will turn into emeralds,
or the rust on tin will sprout a few peach blossoms.
Let grease weave a layer of fine silk-gauze, and
mold steam out a few red-glowing clouds.

Let the dead water ferment into a ditch of green wine,
floating with pearls of white foam;
but the laughter of small pearls turning into large pearls
is broken by spotted mosquitoes stealing the wine.

Thus a ditch of hopelessly dead water
can yet claim a bit of something bright.
And if the frogs can't endure the utter solitude,
let the dead water burst into song.

Here is a ditch of hopelessly dead water.

Here beauty can never reside.

You might as well let ugliness come and cultivate it,

and see what kind of world comes out.

Perhaps

Perhaps you have wept and wept, and can weep no more.
Perhaps. Perhaps you ought to sleep a bit;
then don't let the nighthawk cough, the frogs
croak, or the bats fly.

Don't let the sunlight open the curtain onto your eyes.
Don't let a cool breeze brush your eyebrows.
Ah, no one will be able to startle you awake:
I will open an umbrella of dark pines to shelter your sleep.

Perhaps you hear earthworms digging in the mud,
or listen to the root hairs of small grasses sucking up water.
Perhaps this music you are listening to is lovelier
than the swearing and cursing noises of men.

Then close your eyelids, and shut them tight.
I will let you sleep; I will let you sleep.
I will cover you lightly, lightly with yellow earth.
I will slowly, slowly let the ashes of paper money fly.

Miracle

I never wanted the red of fire, the black at midnight
of the Peach Blossom Pool, the mournful melody of the *p'i-p'a,*

or the fragrance of roses. I never loved the stern
pride of the leopard, and no white dove ever had

the beauty I craved. I never wanted any of these things,
but their *crystallization*—a miracle ten thousand

times more rare than them all! But I am famished and harried.
I cannot go without nourishment: even if it is

dregs and chaff, I still have to beg for it. Heaven knows
I do not wish to be like this. I am by no means

so stubborn or stupid. I am simply tired of waiting,
tired of waiting for the miracle to arrive; and

I dare not starve. Ah, who doesn't know of how little worth
is a tree full of singing cicadas, a jug of turbid wine,

or smoky mountain peaks, bright ravines, stars
glittering in the empty sky? It is all so ordinary,

so inexorably dull, and it isn't worth our ecstatic joy,
our crying out the most moving names, or the

longing to cast gold letters and put them in a song.
I also affirm that to let tears come

at the song of an oriole is trivial, ridiculous,
and a waste of time. But who knows? I cannot be otherwise.

I am so famished and harried I take lamb's-quarters
and wild hyssop for fine grain —

                              but there's no harm
in speaking clearly as long as the miracle appears.

Then at once I will cast off the ordinary. I will never
again gaze at a frosted leaf and dream of a spring blossom's

dazzle. I will not waste my strength, peel open
stones, and demand the warmth of white jade.

Give me one miracle, and I will never again whip ugliness,
and compel it to give up the meaning of its

opposite. Actually, I am weary of all this,
and these strained implications are hard to explain.

All I want is one clear word flashing like a Buddhist relic
with fierce light. I want it whole, complete,

shining in full face. I am by no means so stubborn
or stupid; but I cannot see a round fan without

seeing behind it an immortal face. So,
I will wait for as many incarnations as it takes—

since I've made a vow. I don't know how many
incarnations have already passed; but I'll wait

and wait, quietly, for the miracle to arrive.
That day must come! Let lightning strike me,

volcanoes destroy me. Let all hell rise up and crush me!
Am I terrified? No, no wind will blow out

the light in me. I only wish my cast-off body
would turn into ashes. And so what? That, that minutest

fraction of time is a minutest fraction of—
ah, an extraordinary gust, a divine and stellar hush

(sun, moon, and spin of all stars stopped;
time stopped, too)—the most perfectly round peace.

I hear the sound of the door pivoting: and with it
the rustling of a skirt. That is a miracle.

And in the space of a half-open gold door,
you are crowned with a circle of light!

The Last Day

Water sobs and sobs in the bamboo pipe gutter.
Green tongues of banana leaves lick at the windowpanes.
The four surrounding whitewashed walls are receding,
and I alone cannot fill such a large room.

A fire in a bowl burns and burns in my heart.
Silent, I wait for the faraway guest to arrive.
I feed the fire cobwebs, rat droppings,
and also the scaly skins of spotted snakes.

Now the crowing of a cock hastens a heap of ashes.
A gust of dark wind gropes at my mouth.
Ah, the guest is right in front of me!
I close my eyelids then follow him out.

Good Harvest

Last winter,
the agricultural co-op was formed.
Two lovers sowed in this patch of land.
Seeds were sown into the mud.
Love was cultivated in the heart.

This spring,
a delicate rain sprinkles the land.
The tender buds flourish.
The two lovers, shoulder by shoulder,
come to weed.
Now they gaze into each other's eyes,
now bend down, smiling.

The summer has come.
The grains are ripe.
The date of marriage is set.
Who is not envious?
On the land of the co-op
is a harvest of bliss and love.

The Plum Hint

Plums have bloomed, comrades.
Plum blossoms beckon you to come.
The productive team-captain plucks a branch,
and smiles as he walks into the village.

The snow on thousands of hills melted in one night.
A spout of water turns greener than before.
Listen! The cuckoo in the tree
also changes his new tune.

Outside the village, ponds are full,
ditches dug, and millets green.
Inside the village the cows are fat,
horses strong, and carts adorned.
Who is trying the new whip?
The snapping is so strong!

The windows are open in every house.
In every mansion the doors are wide.
Oh, spring has come!
without signs or signals in advance.

Plums have bloomed, comrades.

The plum gardens crimson like clouds.

O you thousands of full-blooming plums

are like the ten thousand hearts of our commune members.

On the Willow Bank

The riverbank is white like silver.
The morning moon, shaped like
a gold sickle, is standing on the snow.
The willows on both shores
are cast against thousands of clouds.
The traveling bells ring quick—
like beans jumping in the frying pan.

Bells ring quick, bells ring near;
the wheels speed on ahead.
The Red Banners sway in the wind
like peach blossoms in the groves.
The commune's cart is returning;
the snow whirls up to the sky.

O full-laden carts, what do you carry?
Seeds, tools, or fertilizers?
Passersby cannot see well
and stop on the road, asking.

The easing driver
brushes his hands and shrugs—
in a low voice,
"What we carry is spring."

Smiles the one who asks.
Smiles the one who answers.
Their smiles beam like the flashing wheels.
Wheels have trodden a thousand miles
and ahead will keep on flying.

Red Rain

February rain, red rain,
is silently sprinkled on the South Yangtze.
A droplet tints a bone.
A droplet tints a smiling face.

Waters sound "splash splash" outside the village,
and a light rain smoke veils the villagestead.
Children running barefoot—
heads uplifted—run to welcome the drops of rain.

Young men gather round the commune gate
and finger the blade of the brand-new plow.
Everyone tries to plow the first furrow,
and all forget to wear their palm ponchos.

The tractor driver
again and again tries his new combine.
He continues to gaze at the unceasing rain
which dances in circles in front of the windows.

A droplet tints a bone.

A droplet tints a smiling face.

February rain, red rain,

is silently spread on the South Yangtze.

Notes to Poems

RETURN TO CHIANG VILLAGE
li: a Chinese mile, about one-third of a Western mile.

NIGHT AT THE TOWER
Lying-Dragon and Leaping-Horse are epithets for Chu-ke
Liang and Kung-sun Shu, two famous Han-dynasty generals.

FLYING LIGHT
The allusions in "Flying Light" are extremely difficult. In this
poem, the speaker laments the brevity of life and wants to slay
the dragon that draws the sun across the sky, to stop time and
recover peace. He considers the use of elixirs (yellow gold,
white jade) to become an immortal ineffectual and derides Liu
Ch'e (Emperor Wu-ti of the Han) and Ying Cheng (the First
Emperor of Ch'in) for their attempts to build massive, grandi-
ose tombs and immortalize themselves.

There is a story that Ying Cheng died on a journey; his fol-
lowers, anxious to keep his death a secret, filled a carriage with
rotting abalone to disguise the stench of his decomposing body,
then smuggled his corpse back into the capital.

One commentary says that the Spirit Lady was worshiped
by the Han emperor and that the Great Unity was the supreme
deity of the Taoists. I think the speaker is searching for ultimate
knowledge and believes the Spirit Lady has it.

The Jo tree is a mythical tree in the far west, whose foliage
is supposed to glow red at sunset. Intriguingly, Li Ho places the
Jo tree in the east.

Jen Hung-tzu appears to be an immortal; the emperors are "just a heap of bones," whereas Jen Hung-tzu, an utter unknown, has somehow achieved the transcendence that they sought.

SONG OF THE COLLATOR'S SWORD IN THE SPRING BUREAU
Another challenging poem. I think it is essentially an ode to the sword and its power.

Li Ho's elder cousin was employed as a collator in the Spring Bureau, secretariat of the household of the Crown Prince. Ching Ko tried to assassinate the First Emperor of Ch'in. Indigo Field was famous for its jade. Liu Pang, founder of the Han dynasty, killed a snake; that night in a dream, an old woman appeared, cried, and said that he had unwittingly killed her son, the White King of the West.

AUTUMN COMES
Li Ho despairs that his work will not be recognized in his life-time: "Who will ever read the green bamboo slips of this book?" Yet he believes that his work may be uncovered a thousand years later and that his poems will be transformed into green jade.

Before the invention of paper, books were written on slips of bamboo that were bound together. Pao Chao was a fifth-century poet whose poem "Graveyard Lament" was obsessed with mortality. In the *Chuang Tzu,* there's an anecdote about a man who was unjustly put to death: three years after his buri-al, his blood had miraculously turned into green jade.

THE BROCADE ZITHER
There are many commentaries on this famous poem by Li Shang-yin. Presence and absence, dream and reality, the solid

and the insubstantial: the poem uses these polarities to explore the memory of love. Behind the first line, there's a story that the musical instrument, the *chin se,* originally had fifty strings; but when the Chou emperor listened to the music, he found it unbearably sad and ordered that the instrument be broken in half. In the third line, there's a reference to the *Chuang Tzu:* Chuang Tzu once dreamed he was a butterfly; when he woke up, he didn't know if he was Chuang Tzu who dreamed he was a butterfly or a butterfly who dreamed he was Chuang Tzu. In the fourth line, there's another story: Wang-ti, King of Shu, committed adultery and died of shame; after his death, his soul was transformed into the cuckoo.

Mount Lan-t'ien, Indigo Field, was famous for its jade; it is said that the sun creates amazing visions there. These visions, however, can only be seen from far away; up close, they dissolve like smoke.

UNTITLED (1)

In this veiled love poem, the first two lines reveal the situation, but then lines three and four show that the poet is as powerless to prevent the beauty of his beloved from passing as flowers from withering. In lines five and six, the famous phrase, "A spring silkworm spins silk / up to the instant of death," may be read as an image of a poet spinning poems up to the moment of death; it can also be read as an image of endless longing, and the phrases "silkworm" and "silk thread" contain homonyms for "love spasms" and "amorous thoughts." In lines nine and ten, the poet imagines his lover sitting alone in front of a mirror—she is near and yet so far away.

P'eng Mountain is the legendary mountain in the Eastern

Sea. The Green Bird is a messenger of the Queen Mother of the West. At the end of this poem, the speaker's longing reaches out to the infinite.

TO THE TUNE OF "MEETING HAPPINESS"
wu tung trees: Mathews's *Chinese-English Dictionary* says, "A tree, *Sterculia platanifolia;* it is sometimes called the national tree of China; the trunk is straight and beautifully green; it is said to be the only tree on which the phoenix will rest."

EVENING BELL AT A MISTY TEMPLE
dhyana: in Buddhism, a fixed state of contemplation.

MIRACLE
p'i-p'a: a musical instrument, known as the balloon-guitar.

Biographical Notes

T'AO CH'IEN (365–427) is one of the great early poets. He was the first to celebrate the joys of drinking wine, and the illuminations that thereby came to him. He once worked as libationer for his district but soon resigned. He was then offered a job as keeper of records but also turned it down. T'ao was always dissatisfied with official appointments and found, instead, contentment in his "fields and gardens."

WANG HAN (687–726) passed the imperial examinations in 710 C.E. Little else is known about him.

WANG WEI (701–761) was a great poet, painter, and musician. He is best known for his highly condensed and powerful *chüeh-chü* (quatrains). His late work, *The Wang River Sequence,* has still not been fully appreciated for its remarkable combination of lyric, dramatic, and symbolic elements that form an interior journey.

LI PO (701–762) was a free spirit who was once called "an immortal banished to earth." His poems reveal a strong Taoist influence and are remarkable for their lyric flow, spontaneity, and emotional power. According to legend, one night he leaned out of a boat to embrace the moon on the Yangtze River and fell in and drowned.

TU FU (712–770) wrote brilliant poems in the *lü-shih* (regulated verse) form. These poems are amazing for their incised language and tonal counterpoint. For many years he struggled without success to pass through the official examination system. He experienced imprisonment, exile, and dire poverty.

PO CHÜ-I (772–846) is best known for such long poems as *Song of Unending Sorrow* and *Ballad of the P'i-p'a*. His work has a lovely colloquial tone and has been extensively translated by Arthur Waley.

LIU TSUNG-YÜAN (773–819) helped renovate classical Chinese prose. "Snow on the River" is a classic example of *ut pictura poesis*.

LI HO (790–816) wrote rich, complex poems that draw on Chinese shamanism and mythology. He was a child prodigy and, at age seven, stunned Han Yu when he wrote a poem for him, titled "A Tall Official Carriage Comes on a Visit." Each morning, Li Ho galloped on horseback, dashed off rough phrases of poems, and stuffed them in his saddlebag. Later in the day, he would lay out these phrases and incorporate them into poems.

TU MU (803–852) had a long career as a public servant and served near the end of his life in the Grand Secretariat. His poems often express disillusionment and yearn for a former golden era.

LI SHANG-YIN (813–858) tried to pursue a career through the examination system but was blocked by numerous political rivalries and power struggles near the end of the T'ang dynasty. His untitled poems are some of the great love poems in classical Chinese.

LI YÜ (937–978) wrote remarkable poems in the *tz'u* (lyric) genre. He was the last ruler of the Southern T'ang; on his forty-first birthday, the Sung emperor sent him a gift of poisoned wine.

SU TUNG-P'O (1036–1101) was a distinguished calligrapher and painter as well as poet. He served as an administrator but fell into disfavor when he wrote the emperor a letter describing hardships his policies were causing. He was later imprisoned, released, and banished.

LI CH'ING-CHAO (1084–1151) is generally considered to be China's finest woman poet. She was a master of the *tz'u* (lyric) genre and was a painter, calligrapher, and, along with her husband, an avid collector and specialist in ancient stone and bronze inscriptions. Her happy years turned to tragedy, however, when in 1127 their house was destroyed by invading Tartars, and in 1129 her husband contracted typhoid fever and died.

MA CHIH-YÜAN (1260–1324) was an outstanding poet and playwright of the Yuan dynasty. Ma's *Autumn in the Palace of the Han* is a remarkable play that culminates in a moving depiction of the final autumnal desolation of an emperor. Ma also wrote many songs and song cycles. The four poems translated here are in the *ch'ü* (song) form.

SHEN CHOU (1427–1509) was a great painter, calligrapher, and poet of the Ming dynasty. He shunned an official career and instead lived at home taking care of his mother, who lived to be almost one hundred. He enjoyed fame as an artist and teacher.

CHU TA, PA-TA-SHAN-JEN (1626–1705) was a descendant of the Ming imperial family but became a monk after the Manchu invasion led to the collapse of the Ming in 1644. In 1680 he became, or pretended to become, mad, dumb, and given to fits of laughing and weeping. From about 1685 on, he signed all his paintings Pa-ta-shan-jen, "Mountain Man of the Eight Greats." Ch'an Buddhism was a strong influence on his work. The poems translated here are all taken from his paintings.

WEN I-TO (1899–1946) was a pivotal figure in early-twentieth-century Chinese poetry. He rejected classical Chinese, chose to write in the vernacular, and yet his work shows a confluence of the two. He came to the United States, studied at the Art Institute of Chicago and at Colorado College. When he returned to China, he became involved in the political turmoil of his time. On July 15, 1946, Wen gave an impassioned speech denouncing the Kuomintang government and was assassinated later that day.

YEN CHEN (twentieth century) published the poems I have translated in a Szechwan party newspaper in the late 1950s. Although these poems have terminology like "comrades," they harken all the way back to the very first anthology of Chinese poetry, the Shih Ching (The Book of Songs).

About the Translator

Arthur Sze is a second-generation Chinese American who was born in New York City in 1950. He graduated Phi Beta Kappa from the University of California at Berkeley and is the author of seven books of poetry: *The Silk Dragon: Translations from the Chinese* (Copper Canyon Press, 2001), *The Redshifting Web: Poems 1970–1998* (Copper Canyon, 1998), *Archipelago* (Copper Canyon, 1995), *River River* (Lost Roads, 1987), *Dazzled* (Floating Island, 1982), *Two Ravens* (1976; revised edition, Tooth of Time, 1984), *The Willow Wind* (1972; revised edition, Tooth of Time, 1981). His poems have appeared in numerous magazines and anthologies and have been translated into Chinese, Italian, and Turkish. He has conducted residencies at Brown University, Bard College, Naropa Institute, and is the recipient of an Asian American Literary Award, a Balcones Poetry Prize, a Lila Wallace–Reader's Digest Writer's Award, a John Simon Guggenheim Memorial Foundation Fellowship, an American Book Award, a Lannan Literary Award for Poetry, three Witter Bynner Foundation for Poetry Fellowships, two National Endowment for the Arts Creative Writing Fellowships, a George A. and Eliza Gardner Howard Foundation Fellowship, a New Mexico Arts Division Interdisciplinary Grant, and the Eisner Prize, University of California at Berkeley. He lives in Pojoaque, New Mexico, with his wife, Carol Moldaw, and is a Professor of Creative Writing at the Institute of American Indian Arts.

The Chinese character for poetry is made up of two parts: "word" and "temple." It also serves as pressmark for Copper Canyon Press.

Founded in 1972, Copper Canyon Press remains dedicated to publishing poetry exclusively, from Nobel laureates to new and emerging authors. The press thrives with the generous patronage of readers, writers, booksellers, librarians, teachers, students, and funders—everyone who shares the conviction that poetry invigorates the language and sharpens our appreciation of the world.

PUBLISHER'S CIRCLE

Allen Foundation for the Arts

Elliott Bay Book Company

Mimi Gardner Gates

Jaech Family Fund

Lannan Foundation

Rhoady and Jeanne Marie Lee

Lila Wallace–Reader's Digest Fund

National Endowment for the Arts

Port Townsend Paper Company

U.S.–Mexico Fund for Culture

Emily Warn and Daj Oberg

Washington State Arts Commission

The Witter Bynner Foundation

Charles and Barbara Wright

For information and catalogs:

COPPER CANYON PRESS

Post Office Box 271

Port Townsend, Washington 98368

360/385-4925

poetry@coppercanyonpress.org

www.coppercanyonpress.org

The book interior is set in Spectrum,
designed by Jan van Krimpen in the 1940s.
Book design by Valerie Brewster, Scribe Typography.
Printed on archival-quality Glatfelter Author's Text
at McNaughton & Gunn, Inc.